EXPLORING
CAREERS

Careers in Information Technology

Christine Wilcox

ReferencePoint
Press®

San Diego, CA

© 2015 ReferencePoint Press, Inc.
Printed in the United States

For more information, contact:
ReferencePoint Press, Inc.
PO Box 27779
San Diego, CA 92198
www.ReferencePointPress.com

LIBRARY OF CONGRESS CATALOGING-IN-PUBLICATION DATA

Wilcox, Christine.
  Careers in information technology / Christine Wilcox.
    pages cm. — (Exploring careers series)
  Includes bibliographical references and index.
  ISBN-13: 978-1-60152-706-6 (hardback)
  ISBN-10: 1-60152-706-3 (hardback)
  1. Information technology—Vocational guidance—Juvenile literature. 2. Computer science—Vocational guidance—Juvenile literature. I. Title.
  T58.5.W55 2015
  004.023—dc23
                                                    2014014192

Careers in Information Technology

Other titles in the *Exploring Careers* series include:

Contents

The Fastest-Growing Industry

The information technology (IT) industry is changing faster than ever before. Computers now help with everything from designing transportation systems to performing delicate surgeries, and the Internet has given rise to new business sectors like cloud computing and mobile application development. Trained IT professionals are in high demand, especially those who are experienced in the newest technologies. IT was one of the few industries to weather the recent recession (which officially began in December 2007 and ended in mid-2009) with a job loss of only 1 percent. The Bureau of Labor Statistics (BLS) predicts that employment in IT will grow three times faster than in all other industries and that one out of every two jobs in science, technology, engineering, and math will be in computing.

Salaries are also consistently higher in the IT field than they are in other industries. According to Code.org, a nonprofit dedicated to expanding participation in computer science education, computer science is the highest-paid college degree. In 2012 the mean annual salary for IT professionals was $80,180.

A Shortage of Qualified Workers

One reason that wages are high is that there is a shortage of qualified workers in the IT field. "Extended job vacancies have caused one in four companies to lose revenue, so the skills gap is a very real concern," explains Matt Ferguson, chief executive officer (CEO) of CareerBuilder. He tells *Forbes*, "Forty-five percent of Human Resource managers reported that they have open positions for which they can't find qualified candidates." In fact, many companies have to recruit candidates from overseas to fill their highly skilled—and high-paying—computer jobs because less than 2.4 percent of college students in the United States graduate with a degree in computer science. It is estimated that by 2020 there will be 1 million more jobs than there are students enrolled in computer science programs. College students who do pursue computer science or related degrees have an excellent chance of landing a high-paying job after graduation.

Specializing in technology can also lead to a variety of exciting and fascinating careers. Students who study technology become game testers, code breakers, drone pilots, computer-generated imagery engineers, Formula One race car systems designers, gadget reviewers, medical imaging designers, geographic information system mapping engineers, mobile device designers, entrepreneurs, and even astronauts. There are also ample opportunities for IT professionals to work as consultants, and those who are proficient in emerging technologies can essentially write their own job descriptions.

Five Major Areas of Study

For students interested in a career in computers, there are in general five different majors available at most universities and colleges:

Computer engineering: Computer engineers design everything from silicon chips and smartphones to global communication systems and laser surgery tools. They often work with cutting-edge technologies such as artificial intelligence, nanotechnology, and 3-D virtual reality. Students who enjoy inventing or building computerized devices should consider pursuing this degree.

Computer science: Computer scientists love to solve puzzles, and their jobs are often about designing software solutions to real-world problems. They develop innovative software products such as search engines and operating systems. Students who are creative and enjoy solving problems using math should consider this degree.

Information Technology: Job Growth Forecast, 2010–2020

Job title	May 2010 employment	2020 jobs forecast	Job growth forecast	Pct job growth forecast	Expected growth rate thru 2020	May 2010 median wage
Software developers, systems software	392,300	519,400	127,100	32%	Much faster than average	$94,180
Database administrators	110,800	144,800	34,000	31%	Much faster than average	$73,490
Network & computer system admins	347,300	443,800	96,500	28%	Faster than average	$69,160
Software developers, applications	520,800	664,500	143,700	28%	Faster than average	$87,790
Computer systems analyst	544,400	664,800	120,400	22%	Faster than average	$77,740
Information security analysts, Web developers, and computer network architects	302,300	367,900	65,600	22%	Faster than average	$75,660
Computer & information systems managers	307,900	363,700	55,800	18%	About average	$115,780
Computer support specialists	607,100	717,100	110,000	18%	About average	$46,260
Computer programmers	363,100	406,800	43,700	12%	About average	$71,380

Source: US Bureau of Labor Statistics, *Occupational Outlook Handbook*, 2012. www.bls.gov/ooh.

Software engineering: Software engineers, also known as software developers, specialize in the design and development of software. Software engineering classes are often offered within a computer science program, but some colleges offer software engineering as a separate degree. Students who are specifically interested in developing software should consider specializing in software engineering.

Information systems: Information systems specialists focus on bridging the gap between technology and business. This major is normally available within business schools and can also be called management information systems, computer information systems, or business information systems. This degree is ideal for students who are interested in learning how computers can make organizations more effective.

Information technology: Although *information technology* is the catch-all term for computer-related technologies, information technology is also a specific career path. IT specialists design and support an organization's IT infrastructure (the hardware and software designed by computer engineers, computer scientists, and software engineers). IT specialists often support organizations by selecting computer systems, designing the company website, and troubleshooting users' problems. Students who love working with computers and enjoy helping people should consider a degree in information technology.

Computer Literacy in the Modern World

Computers have become integrated into nearly every facet of modern life, and few industries exist that are not at least somewhat dependent on IT. Seventy percent of IT jobs are not in the IT sector; they are in a variety of areas, including manufacturing, retail, the arts, financial services, and even weather forecasting. For instance, in health care, health informatics is a hot new field. As hospitals convert to electronic health record systems, people who have both medical knowledge and experience in programming or database management are in high demand.

Students who do not pursue a career in IT are still well advised to understand the basics about information technology. Kirk McDonald, president of an advertising tech company in Manhattan, writes in the *Wall Street Journal* that he has a hard time finding graduates who even understand what computer engineers and programmers do. "I'm not going to hire you unless you can at least understand the basic way my company works," he says. "If you want a job in media, technology or a related field . . . teach yourself just enough of the grammar and the logic of computer languages to be able to see the big picture." According to many experts, developing computer literacy will give nearly every new graduate an advantage in the job market.

Social Media Specialist

Dozens of social media–related job titles have flooded employment websites in the past few years. Among the most common are social media strategist, online community manager, search engine optimization specialist, and social media marketing coordinator. In April 2014 a search for the keywords *social media* on the online jobs site Indeed.com returned almost forty-six thousand jobs. It seems as if every business is trying to use social media to improve sales and customer relations. However, the role of the social media specialist is so new that there is little consensus about what skills a specialist needs—or even what the job actually entails. Although this can be confusing for those who are interested in pursuing a career in social media, it also means that job seekers can help define their own jobs.

The most basic task of a social media specialist is to maintain and expand a company's social

At a Glance:
Social Media Specialist

Minimum Educational Requirements
Bachelor's degree or equivalent

Personal Qualities
Excellent people skills; interest in social media; strong written communication skills

Certification and Licensing
None

Working Conditions
Indoors

Salary Range
About $31,860 to $45,373

Number of Jobs
As of 2012 about 229,100*

Future Job Outlook
Growth rate of 12 percent through 2022*

*Numbers are for public relations specialists, a group that includes social media specialists.

networking presence. However, even an entry-level social media specialist is usually tasked with much more. Some specialists are part of the marketing department; their job is to generate interest in a product or service through social networking posts, campaigns, contests, and so on. Other specialists are part of the customer service or public relations departments. They create, foster, and sometimes host online communities, field questions about products and complaints, and generate goodwill toward the company. Still others are bloggers, who provide regular content to readers interested in a topic related to a product.

Social media specialists typically start their day before leaving for work; they check their e-mails and social media notifications to gauge the success of the content posted on the previous day. At work they respond to all of the questions and comments they have received on the various social media platforms they monitor, as well as catch up on any forum discussions they are taking part in. They usually employ monitoring software to track mentions of the organization across networks so they can keep abreast of the general sentiment their company is generating. Then they review the material slated for posting that day and determine the best way to release it. Sarah Mincher, a social media specialist, explains that there are best practices to follow when releasing content. "For example, the way I'd release a new article on Linkedin will be completely different than the time and delivery of how I'll tweet that same article later on in the day," she writes in DigitalSherpa, a social media marketing website. "When it comes to posting on social media, one size, or uh, post, does not fit all." After a posting schedule is set, a specialist will spend the rest of the workday writing content, monitoring active media platforms, and giving feedback to other departments. Specialists often continue monitoring and interacting on social media well into the evening. Mincher says, "The Internet never takes a break, and, in a way, this means I can't either."

Social media specialists need to understand basic business principles and be able to quantify the return on investment of their media campaigns. Usually, just increasing the number of "likes" or page clicks does nothing for a company's bottom line. Specialists need to understand brand management principles, the psychology behind Internet memes (humorous ideas that spread quickly, often via social media), and the way that personal interactions affect how a company is perceived by the public. They also must know about Internet marketing strategies and search engine optimization (the practice of using keywords and links to increase the likelihood that content will be returned by a search engine). The more specialists know about the business of online interaction, the more valuable they will be in the job market.

Social media specialists usually concentrate on one or two knowledge areas to set themselves apart. Some specialists focus on advertising, others on customer service. And while all social media specialists must write well and enjoy writing often, many focus on generating great content. Specialists can also focus on analyzing and interpreting the vast amount of data social media sites generate.

How Do You Become a Social Media Specialist?

Education

Most social media specialists have bachelor's degrees, often in communications or marketing. However, social media specialists can have any educational background as long as they can demonstrate their skills in social media—which always includes strong writing skills. Although most large companies expect job seekers to have a bachelor's degree, they still base their hiring decision on a candidate's online presence and experience.

Volunteer Work and Internships

Interning as a social media assistant or volunteering to assist a company with its social media strategy is the best way to gain the experience needed to land an entry-level job in social media. Students can do this while in college—or even while in high school. Experts suggest that anyone interested in a career in social media first become a super user—or an expert with the most popular social media platforms. Next they should seek an internship or offer to assist a company or nonprofit with their social media strategy for free. That experience can be documented in a personal website or blog, which can itself be marketed through social media. Because a personal website will be one of the first things a prospective employer sees when running an online search on a job candidate, it should double as a résumé, highlighting the applicant's accomplishments and professionalism.

Tracy Brisson, founder of One2Many Consulting, believes that it is crucial for job candidates to quantify their experience in their résumés. She explains that she always starts by asking how the social media community grew during the candidate's tenure. "In an interview, I'll follow up on strategies and approaches used, but without numbers on a resume or LinkedIn profile, it would be hard for me to take an applicant seriously," she tells the website Mashable. Brisson advises that job candidates make sure they quantify what they achieved during an internship with statements like "Increased engagement from an average of 24 comments per week to an average of 75 in a three-month period on our Facebook Page" or "Helped establish a two-fold increase in Twitter traffic to our product page, resulting in a quarterly revenue increase of 50 percent."

Skills and Personality

Social media specialists must love to be social. They must be willing to take the time to develop relationships with the people they interact with online. They must also be in touch with their customers or target audience and know where they congregate and what they like to discuss. Social media specialists are always learning and expanding their skills. They must be curious enough about social media to be willing to learn about it outside of work by following professional blogs, reading articles, and exploring new social network platforms.

Specialists must also have strong writing skills. Especially in entry-level positions, social media specialists spend most of their time generating content. Those with a flair for writing might gravitate toward being content specialists or bloggers, but all specialists must be able to write well. They must also understand that their style reflects the company they represent. Although many young people see nothing wrong with communicating in web speak (shortening words phonetically, like typing "u" for *you*), it may not reflect well on the company's brand. Specialists must also be able to craft what they say with care and sensitivity, to avoid inadvertently insulting a customer. Bloggers, who create online personas, often have more leeway when it comes to inserting humor or sarcasm in their posts, but everyone who represents a company or brand must fully understand the impact their words have on the organization they represent.

Finally, social media specialists must have excellent people skills. Even though they are not interacting face-to-face, it is crucial that they know how to handle complaints, defuse tension, and put a human face on their company. "Exercise empathy at all times," advises Suzanne McDonald, CEO of the online marketing company Designated Editor. "Focus on your audience's needs and desires. If you can do this well, people will respond to you and your brand, which will generate results for your brand and your career."

On the Job

Employers

Any company with a social media presence has the need for a social media specialist. Many small companies task social media monitoring to their marketing departments, but larger companies are getting more sophisticated with their social media strategy. According to a 2013 social business survey by the Altimeter Group, social media was previously an offshoot of marketing and public relation efforts, but now it is becoming integrated across all elements of a typical business, including product development, sales, and retention.

There are also many Internet marketing companies that specialize in social media marketing for their clients. These companies hire people with strong writing skills and advanced social media platform knowledge.

Working Conditions

Social media specialists work indoors, usually in a casual environment. Most monitor social media after hours from their personal devices. Many put in evening hours so that they can join in online conversations or monitor content that is launched in the evening. Some social media specialists are able to telecommute a few days a week.

Earnings

Salaries of social media specialists vary greatly, based on location and skill level. According to a 2012 infographic by Onward Search, specialists in Phoenix, Arizona, earned a low of $30,000, while specialists in New York City earned a high of $71,000. According to Simply Hired, the average salary for all jobs in social media is $55,000.

Opportunities for Advancement

Social media specialists can become strategists or data analysts, advance to management positions, and eventually direct a company's entire social media strategy. However, many companies have not yet defined how social media meshes with business strategies. In these companies it is crucial that specialists take the initiative to grow their own positions. Research by the Altimeter Group shows that there comes a point in the career of a social media specialist when he or she becomes mired in a "help desk" role, overwhelmed by an increasing number of social media requests. It is at this point that social media specialists must push to expand the involvement of social media in the business. The specialist must become a strategist (another common job title in social media) and be able to quantify how specific social media strategies will generate income for the business. If this is not possible, the best career move is probably to switch jobs or companies.

What Is the Future Outlook for Social Media Specialists?

Social media is a rapidly expanding career area that is still undefined. The career networking site LinkedIn includes more than eighteen thousand people who define themselves as "social media gurus." And according to a 2013 social business survey by Altimeter, companies with one hundred thousand employees now report an average of forty-nine full-time employees supporting social media, as compared to twenty in 2010. New York, San Jose, and San Francisco employ the highest volume of people in social media professions.

According to Carrie Kerpen, CEO of the social media agency Likeable Media, interpreting the data social media sites generate is one career area that is expanding. She tells *Forbes*, "There will be an entire new job sector built on understanding the data of social media. Want to get into a complex, exciting field within social? Start there."

Find Out More

Social Media Club
PO Box 14881
San Francisco, CA 94114
website: http://socialmediaclub.org

The Social Media Club's mission is to promote media literacy and standard technologies, encourage ethical behavior, and share best practices among social media professionals. The organization's website contains links to several club blogs and social media events, as well as general educational materials.

Social Media Professional Association
530 Lytton Ave.
Palo Alto, CA 94301
phone: (650) 600-3844
website: www.socialmediaprofessionalassociation.com

The Social Media Professional Association is an organization that provides training, education, and certification in social media marketing. The website contains links to articles and research about social media in a marketing context.

Social Media Today
website: http://socialmediatoday.com

Social Media Today is an independent online community for professionals in public relations, marketing, advertising, and other disciplines that rely on social media. The website hosts lively debates about the tools, platforms, companies, and personalities that are revolutionizing the way information is consumed. Articles are contributed by professionals who work with social media.

Word of Mouth Marketing Association (WOMMA)
65 E. Wacker Place, Suite 500
Chicago, IL 60601
phone: (312) 853-4400
website: www.womma.org

WOMMA is the official trade association dedicated to word-of-mouth and social media marketing. The website contains information about best practices, regulations, and opportunities within digital media. Various online publications are available to nonmembers at no cost, as is WOMMA's industry blog.

Software Tester

What Does a Software Tester Do?

Software testers (also known as quality assurance testers or QA analysts) improve the quality of computer software by testing it in each phase of its development. Each type of software requires a different method of testing to assure quality standards, so testing methods and the qualifications of the tester vary greatly. Some testers need only "soft skills" like attention to detail, ability to work independently, and strong communication skills. Others need to be as knowledgeable as the software developer who created the application. Many people interested in software development or programming start out as testers, whereas others pursue software testing as a career.

A typical day for an entry-level software tester includes spending many hours working alone with software to be tested. Some testers work from home, and others work at a bank of computers with other testers. When a tester finds an error or potential problem, he or she must flag the issue, document it, and alert the software development team. Documentation usually includes a description of the problem as well as an explanation of why it is important and should be fixed. It is crucial that testers employ

At a Glance:
Software Tester

Minimum Educational Requirements
High school diploma

Personal Qualities
Critical thinking; self-directed; strong written communication skills

Certification and Licensing
Suggested

Working Conditions
Indoors

Salary Range
About $45,000 to $89,000

Number of Jobs
As of 2012 about 206,000

Future Job Outlook
Growth rate of 3 to 7 percent through 2022

a certain amount of tact and diplomacy in their documentation or the tester-developer relationship can become adversarial. This is why strong communication skills are so important; testers must describe the problem clearly and succinctly without coloring their documentation with a superior or condescending attitude.

Software testers usually specialize in a specific niche, or type of testing. Some common types of testing are manual, automation, or performance testing. Manual testers take on the role of the end user and attempt to find errors in the software's design. This type of testing can be tedious because it requires the tester to use every feature of the software in every conceivable combination. Skilled manual testers have what some inside the industry refer to as a "test to break" attitude; in other words, they deliberately stress the software to reveal any hidden bugs. Manual testers must also be able to think like an end user. If the software is frequently used by people without strong computer skills, the tester must anticipate mistakes users might make and note any user interface issues that might confuse them. Automation testers run—and sometimes write—scripts that automate many of the software's operations. This is a time-saving and cost-effective way of testing software, but it sometimes requires that testers have scripting and programming skills. Performance testing uses automation to test the ability of the software to perform under heavy workloads. Performance testers evaluate the software's responsiveness, its capacity, and so on.

Individuals with excellent communication skills and a facility with computers can find entry-level software testing jobs right out of high school, especially in the gaming industry. However, most employers require entry-level testers to have at least an undergraduate certificate in software testing or a bachelor's degree. Some also expect testers to have experience with testing software like Selenium, an understanding of testing methodologies, and basic programming skills. Advanced testers who work with complex software must have in-depth analytical and technical skills, advanced knowledge of testing software and methodologies, and an understanding of the entire software development process. Senior testing manager Nigel Edwards gave this advice in a Software Testing Club online discussion: "Take the time to study and absorb programming concepts, and also to learn a programming language. . . . Continue to keep pace with development languages; in other words, learn your first language (which will grant you a good base in terms of understanding logic and general programming principles) but then continue to keep abreast of developments as and when they arise."

How Do You Become a Software Tester?

Education

There are many routes to becoming a software tester. Some experts claim that there are no specific educational requirements for software testers, but more and more employers are requiring at least some formal study. Technical and community colleges offer undergraduate certificates in software quality assurance. These programs can be completed in as little as six months, include hands-on training, and prepare certificate holders for entry-level positions in software testing. However, those who hold certificates can face steep competition for jobs from individuals with bachelor's degrees. Those who want a career in software testing usually get a bachelor's degree in computer science, information technology, or software engineering, and some programs offer specialization in quality assurance. About 64 percent of software testers have a bachelor's degree, 14 percent have an associate's degree, and 14 percent have a master's degree. Students who want to advance but do not want to pursue a master's degree can find graduate certificate programs in software quality assurance. These can be completed in as little as one year while the student works a full-time job, and course credit can sometimes be transferred toward a master's degree. Master's degree programs are usually in software engineering with a concentration on testing issues.

Education does not stop after employment. Technology is advancing more quickly than ever before, and skill sets quickly become irrelevant. Software testing consultant Anne-Marie Charrett advises software testers to keep up-to-date with what is happening in their field and to learn from the testing community. "You need to be committed to keeping yourself relevant," she writes in her blog, *Maverick Tester*. "Contributing to the community is a great way of meeting local and international people and you learn so much. . . . Online networking is important too because it allows you to connect with like minded people, plus its a great source of learning."

Certification

Many employers require software testers to be certified. One of the most popular testing certifications is the Certified Tester Foundation Level from the International Software Testing Qualifications Board. Requirements for certification include passing a written exam and accumulating a combination of education and experience. Training programs are available to help students prepare to take certification exams, and some employers pay for training. Testers can also be certified in various testing and software products such as Selenium, a browser automation tool used in testing web-based applications.

Volunteer Work and Internships

While there are few volunteer opportunities for software testers, internships are commonly offered to college students who want to pursue a career in software testing. These internships give students valuable experience that can help them enter the job market at a higher level than those who have no experience. High school students who have advanced computer programming skills may also find software testing internships, particularly in the gaming industry.

Skills and Personality

Software testing attracts a specific type of individual. Just like editors appreciate good writing, software testers appreciate well-designed software, and they enjoy helping developers improve that software. They are curious, patient, thorough, and can work for long stretches without direct supervision. Testers should be analytical enough to be able to uncover the source of a software problem and have strong enough written communication skills to describe that problem clearly and accurately. It is helpful if testers can analyze a problem from both a developer's and an end user's point of view. The best testers have a good grasp of the entire software development process while also being able to step into an end user's shoes. To advance their careers, testers must be willing to add to their knowledge through self-study and professional development.

Employers

While some software testers are contract workers who move from project to project, most are either hired directly or are placed in long-term assignments by IT recruiting firms. Software testers work for software companies, large organizations that have a quality assurance unit in their IT department, or any company that has a software component.

Working Conditions

A software tester usually works independently in an office environment. Some testers are able to work from home and telecommute at least a few days a week. Most testers work full time. Since software development is often deadline driven, it is not uncommon for testers to work long hours. In addition, some automated testing scripts must run for several hours and then be checked before the next phase of testing can begin. This means that testers occasionally must work the night shift.

Earnings

The salary of software testers depends on the type of software they are testing and the skills and experience they need to provide quality assurance. At one end of the spectrum are games testers, who earn about $12 per hour and rarely advance to more senior level positions. At the other end are quality assurance engineers, who earn about $97,000 per year and up. The BLS groups software testers in with computer systems analysts, who earned a median salary of $79,680 in 2012; however, these specialized systems analysts typically do in-depth testing of the systems they design.

According to information gathered by Indeed.com in March 2014, typical software testers make an average of $76,000 per year. Junior software testers make about $45,000 and senior software testers about $89,000 annually. Two national IT staffing companies, Robert Half Technology and Modis, reported similar figures. Modis found that in 2013, testers with fewer than two years' experience earned $46,758, those with two to four years' experience earned $49,153, and those with five or more years' experience earned $51,738 a year. Robert Half Technology found that testing managers earned between $83,250 and $111,000 a year in 2013 and predict that software testers will see about a 5 percent increase in salary in 2014.

Opportunities for Advancement

As software testers gain more experience, they can expect to advance to more senior-level positions. Those who wish to work in management typically need more education, such as some graduate-level management courses. Software testers who have advanced testing skills can become software test engineers. These testing professionals are often skilled software developers who write complex testing scripts to test specialized software. They must have at least a bachelor's degree in computer science or software engineering as well as graduate certifications in testing. Many also have master's degrees. Software engineers often work for cutting-edge technology companies and are an integral part of all phases of software development.

What Is the Future Outlook for Software Testers?

There is a trend in the software development industry to outsource less-complex software testing or to automate it, which results in fewer entry-level software testing jobs. According to Charrett, "The fact is, there are less testing jobs out there. That doesn't mean there are less quality testing jobs though. While its [sic] true that the crumbs from the table need to be shared among more, there is still plenty of meat and gravy at the table." Skilled testers with current skills and a strong understanding of the software development process can typically find high-paying jobs. Many work for leading technology companies like Intel, Cisco Systems, and Google.

Find Out More

Association for Software Testing (AST)
website: www.associationforsoftwaretesting.org

The AST is an international nonprofit professional association with members in more than fifty countries. The AST is dedicated to advancing the understanding of the science and practice of software testing. Its website contains user forums, an industry blog, and various training materials.

SoftwareQATest.com
website: http://softwareqatest.com

SoftwareQATest.com is a website developed and maintained by an experienced software testing consultant to help educate the software testing community about various tools and techniques. The website is also geared toward anyone who has an interest in software quality assurance. It contains links to organizations, training materials, articles, and other information about software testing.

Software Test Professionals (STP)
1115 Elkton Dr., Suite 301
Colorado Springs, CO 80907
phone: (877) 257-9531
website: www.softwaretestpro.com

STP provides testing professionals with information, education, and professional networking opportunities. The website contains articles, case studies, and best practices related to software testing. The association also publishes *Software Test and Quality Assurance*, a leading industry magazine.

Successful Quality Assurance
website: www.successful-quality-assurance.com

Successful Quality Assurance is a full-service software testing company that also provides a wealth of educational materials about software testing. Its website contains articles and free courses on software testing fundamentals and techniques.

Website Developer

With today's user-friendly authoring tools, almost anyone can design a website to blog about a hobby or advertise a small business. But to do more, it is usually necessary to seek the services of a website developer—or web developer, as it is more commonly known. Web developers design and program complex websites. They work for online companies like Amazon and Facebook, large organizations like universities or state governments, or any group that wants to build a complex, interactive website. Web developers have an in-depth understanding of how the Internet works and keep abreast of current online technologies and innovations. According to Nelly Yusupova, chief technology officer of the networking group Webgrrls International, "Web development is very exciting, demanding and fun. You have the best of both worlds, where you get to exercise your creativity and have the exacting demands of coding. You always have to be learning and have the ability to learn on the fly."

Some web developers handle all phases of website development and maintenance, but many specialize in either the front end (what the user sees)

At a Glance:
Website Developer

Minimum Educational Requirements
High school diploma

Personal Qualities
Creative problem solving; detail oriented

Certification and Licensing
Voluntary

Working Conditions
Indoors

Salary Range
About $33,500 to $105,200

Number of Jobs
As of 2013 about 136,900 to 141,400

Future Job Outlook
Growth rate of 20 percent through 2022

or the back end (the behind-the-scenes programming and architecture that makes the site work). Those who specialize in front end development focus on creating aesthetically pleasing websites that are intuitively user-friendly. Front end developers work closely with an organization's stakeholders (those who have a stake in the outcome of the project) to translate their vision into a unified design. They have a strong understanding of aesthetics, graphic design, and user interface principles. They use web development and graphic design tools like Dreamweaver, Photoshop, and Illustrator, and they are fluent in web programming languages like Hypertext Markup Language (HTML) and Cascading Style Sheets (CSS). Many work extensively with images, sound, and video.

Web developers who specialize in back end development design and program the underlying structure that makes a website functional. They work closely with the front end developer to bring the client's vision to life. Back end developers write code in multiple programming languages such as JavaScript and Structured Query Language (SQL), create interfaces to relational databases and other websites, and design interactive elements using multimedia platforms like Flash. They also test the performance and capacity of the site, making sure it works equally well on all web browsers and meets security standards.

Web developers who specialize primarily in the front end of development are often known as web designers. Those who specialize in the back end are sometimes known as web architects. However, these three terms—*designer*, *developer*, and *architect*—are often used interchangeably both inside and outside the industry. For this reason, it is important for those considering a career in web development to understand the difference between front end and back end work. Developers who specialize in front end work have a strong interest in art and design. Those who specialize in back end programming love to solve problems with computers and have a facility with math. Some front end and back end developers team up and start their own businesses.

Although web developers tend to focus on either front end or back end development, most can do both—though often not equally well. However, having strengths in both areas can be extremely useful, especially since many employers do not understand the difference. As

Cory LaViska, founder of the web development company A Beautiful Site, writes in his blog, "In this industry it is very clear that, despite a reasonable separation of roles and responsibilities, an individual's job title is not always a reflection of their personal expertise. It is, alas, more often an indication of their position in terms of demand and naivety." In other words, it is common for a back end web developer to have the title of web designer (and vice versa) simply because the company he or she works for does not know that these titles reflect two very different skill sets. For this reason, job seekers should read job descriptions carefully to understand if the position requires a specialization in creative design, technical programming, or both.

How Do You Become a Website Developer?

Education

The educational requirements of a web developer vary. Many developers are judged only by their portfolios—or the websites that they have created in the past. This is particularly true if a developer specializes in front end design and is looking for employment with a small company. Many front end developers have a degree in art or graphic design, though it is possible to find employment with a strong portfolio and a high school diploma. Larger companies usually require that front end developers have at least an associate's degree in website development or a related field. Developers specializing in the more technical back end programming are often required to have a bachelor's degree—preferably in computer science or a related field.

All web developers need to be fluent in HTML. Most employers usually require several other programming languages, as well as facility with multimedia publishing tools. Many web developers take classes in a variety of computer languages and tools throughout their career. Because Internet technology changes so quickly, education must be ongoing.

Certification

Certification in website development or design is available by various organizations. Developers can also get certified in computer

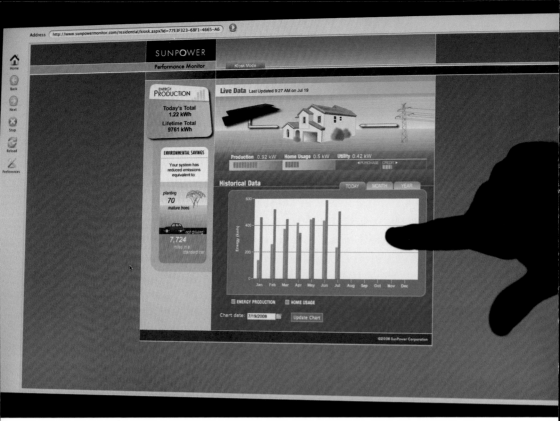

Websites have become crucial sales and marketing tools for businesses of all types, spurring demand for skilled website developers. Developers design and program websites, often building in a wide variety of interactive and user-friendly features.

languages and tools. Certification usually costs several hundred dollars and entails self-study and successful completion of an exam. For instance, the World Wide Web Consortium offers free study materials and low-cost certifications in HTML, CSS, and various other web authoring tools and programming languages. Companies such as Adobe also offer certifications in their products, such as the web development tool Dreamweaver.

Volunteer Work and Internships

Internships and volunteer work are an excellent way for high school students to find out if website development is a good fit. Many students have already created one or more websites on their own time and are knowledgeable enough to volunteer to design or redesign the website of a local nonprofit. Internships are also widely available and are an excellent way to learn new skills and network with professionals in the field. While some students may be talented enough to charge for their services, accepting an unpaid internship with an innovative company can be more educational than a paying job—and more valuable, in terms of making contacts in the industry.

Skills and Personality

Web developers must be passionate about the Internet and have a keen interest in exploring its capabilities. Because technology changes so quickly, it is crucial that developers stay abreast of innovations in the field. The best developers are lifelong learners who practice their craft regardless of whether or not they are paid to do so.

Though web developers must be creative thinkers and excellent problem solvers, they also must be extremely detail oriented. There is no room for error when writing code, and a single misplaced character can shut down an entire website. Even though website development is creative work, it is also methodical and time-consuming. Developers must be able to concentrate for long stretches of time, often in isolation.

Finally, web developers must be able to communicate effectively with their clients—whether those clients are paying customers or stakeholders inside a company. Developers must be able to understand their clients' needs and translate their vision. Many developers are also required to provide at least some website content, so strong written communication skills are also important.

Employers

Many web developers are contract workers employed by IT consulting companies. A project with a consulting company can last anywhere from a few weeks to several years. Contract work usually pays more than full-time employment, but benefits such as vacation and retirement usually are not included. Some consulting companies hire developers on a full-time basis and move them from project to project.

Permanent web development positions are available with a variety of companies—from small start-ups to very large organizations like hospitals or banks. Web developers also work in the creative services departments of large organizations like universities and state governments. According to Yusupova, the atmosphere in workplaces that employ web developers varies "from a very flexible, hands on, nimble, 'fly by the seat of your pants' environment of a startup and [being] very involved with every aspect of a project, to a very structured environment with more levels of approval and a more bureaucratic approach."

Some web developers are freelance workers or start their own businesses. In 2012 about a quarter of web developers were self-employed. Freelance web developer Jonathan Wold suggests that those who want to go this route specialize in a particular area or niche. "The demand for . . . specialists is high," he writes on the website Under30CEO. "You can focus your efforts on a niche or on a specific facet of development (e.g. design, mobile development, engineering). You can also focus on a geographic region, becoming a specialist to serving businesses in a specific area."

Working Conditions

Web developers work indoors, often in a casual environment. Most developers work full time, and overtime is often required so that deadlines can be met. Some developers must occasionally work the night shift so that a company website can be tested without disrupting operations. Freelance web developers can choose their own hours, and many work part time.

Earnings

According to the BLS, the median annual wage for web developers in 2012 was $62,500. The top 10 percent earned more than $105,200, and the bottom 10 percent earned less than $33,500. Indeed.com lists the average salary as of March 2014 as $88,000 and notes that web developer salaries are 48 percent higher than average salaries in the United States. However, according to *U.S. News & World Report*, even though web developers ranked third on its list of the eleven top technology jobs of 2014 (due to factors like low stress and high flexibility), developers earned less on average than nine of the eleven, surpassing only computer support technicians.

Opportunities for Advancement

Web developers earn less than many IT professionals because there are few opportunities to advance within the discipline. After web developers reach senior status, they typically transition to management positions, heading up creative services departments or moving into project management. Other senior web developers go on to start their own businesses.

What Is the Future Outlook for Website Developers?

According to the BLS, jobs for web developers are projected to grow 20 percent through 2022. This is largely due to projected expansion of e-commerce and the use of mobile devices. However, because there is no way to predict how the Internet will change over the next ten years and what innovations and technologies will emerge, these growth estimates may not be reliable. It is more likely that web developers will transition from desktop and mobile web development to development in entirely new mediums and platforms. Developers who are skilled in multiple programming languages and cutting-edge digital multimedia tools will have the best prospects.

Find Out More

International Webmasters Association (IWA)
119 E. Union St., Suite A
Pasadena, CA 91103
phone: (626) 449-3709
website: http://iwanet.org

The IWA is one of the leading organizations for web professionals. It provides education programs such as its Certified Web Professional program, and it provides its members with professional networking opportunities and educational resources. Its website also contains a list of job profiles and professional standards.

WebDeveloper.com
website: www.webdeveloper.com

WebDeveloper.com is a free online discussion forum that covers all aspects of web development, including client-side and server-side development, design, site management, and business issues. The site is a gathering place for web development professionals to share knowledge and advice and a resource for those new to the field.

Webgrrls International
PO Box 2425
New York, NY 10021
phone: (888) 932-4775
website: www.webgrrls.com

Webgrrls International is an online and offline networking organization of professional women who work with the web. The site includes a networking area, event listings, a jobs bank, an industry blog, and various educational materials. Members include web developers, graphic designers, web content writers, and other web professionals.

Webmonkey
PO Box 37706
Boone, IA 50037
website: www.webmonkey.com

Webmonkey is an online resource for web developers created and hosted by *Wired*. The website includes tutorials, tips, and advice for designing and building websites and programming web applications. It has articles for beginners, professionals, students, bloggers, and programmers of all skill levels.

Database Administrator

According to an old joke, a database administrator (DBA) has three core responsibilities: protect the data, protect the data, and protect the data. Data integrity is the number one responsibility of a DBA—especially today, when so many online companies base their business model on collecting and selling information. Just about every type of retailer uses a database to store and analyze information about customers and products, as do hospitals, banks, insurance companies, governments, and universities. And according to a 2012 study by the Direct Marking Association, online marketers and data brokerage firms have made storing and analyzing data an industry worth $62 billion. Big Data is big business, and the key to its success is the DBA.

DBAs use database management systems such as Oracle and Microsoft SQL Server to store, organize, and protect an organization's data. They work with management to determine an organization's data needs, and then design or customize a database—usually with the help of a database programmer—to meet those needs. DBAs must not only understand the software they use, they must also have an

At a Glance:

Database Administrator

Minimum Educational Requirements
Bachelor's degree

Personal Qualities
Analytical thinker; enjoys problem solving; good communication skills

Certification and Licensing
Suggested

Working Conditions
Indoors

Salary Range
About $42,930 to $118,720

Number of Jobs
As of 2012 about 118,700

Future Job Outlook
Growth rate of 15 percent through 2022

in-depth understanding of computer systems and networks, as well as database theory and design. On a day-to-day basis, some of their tasks include merging old databases into new ones, allocating system storage, monitoring and optimizing performance over a network, planning for backup and recovery of lost data, and ensuring system security.

Keeping the database secure is an extremely important part of a DBA's job. Because personal data can be so valuable—especially if it includes Social Security numbers or credit card information—databases are a prime target of hackers and thieves. DBAs are responsible for monitoring everyone who has access to the database, as well as preventing those who do not have access from breaching the system. Their three main security tasks are authentication, or setting up new user accounts; authorization, or setting up permission profiles, which restrict the areas of the database individuals have access to; and auditing, or tracking who did what inside the database. Auditing is particularly important, and DBAs who work in regulated industries like health care have to adhere to auditing rules and reporting requirements. Because malicious hacking is the largest source of all data breaches, the DBA must also keep all security features of the database up-to-date and coordinate with the network administrator about updating network security software. Hackers often enter databases through the Internet connection, so DBAs with advanced knowledge of network security are particularly valuable to companies that store sensitive or valuable data.

In a smaller office, DBAs often take on many more IT duties than just maintaining the company's database. They sometimes double as the network administrator or have other computer-related duties. Other DBAs must have highly specialized skills, especially if their databases are very large or are in constant use. High-availability databases are those that are accessed not just during working hours but are available via the Internet twenty-four hours a day. In some cases keeping these databases up and running at all times is literally a life-and-death situation, such as the databases that power electronic health record systems used by hospitals. Administrators working with these types of databases must know how to perform maintenance on systems while they are in use, how to plan for redundant hardware and software components in case a portion of the database fails, and so forth. Very large databases (VLDBs) are those that contain a great deal of unstructured data, such as documents, images, and video. Administrators who work with VLDBs must understand special techniques to make the data manageable.

Because the management of data has become so central to so many businesses, DBAs tend to be highly valued members of the management team. "Because of their importance inside organizations, they can be the key driver of success," explains Heidi Golledge, CEO of CareerBliss. In fact, the online jobs site surveyed the reviews of its twenty-five thousand users and found that database administrator was ranked as the number one happiest job. Golledge explained to *Forbes* that DBAs were especially pleased with the quality of their daily tasks and their control over their jobs. Work-life balance, compensation, growth opportunities, and relationships with bosses and coworkers were also measured.

How Do You Become a Database Administrator?

Education

Most DBAs have a bachelor's degree, usually in management information systems. Some have master's degrees that focus study on the management or analysis of data, such as computer science, information systems, or information technology. Other employers prefer a DBA's master's degree be in business with a minor in information systems. DBAs must also understand database language, such as Structured Query Language (SQL). A database query is a set of coded instructions that tells the database what information to retrieve. Understanding how to construct queries is central to working with databases.

More important than formal education is experience. DBAs must first gain experience working with databases for at least one to five years before they can take on the role of administrator. Most start as data analysts, interpreting data for financial firms or market research companies. Others start as database programmers or developers. This experience allows DBAs to become specialists in one or more database management systems such as Oracle or DB2.

Certification

DBAs are expected to be product experts, and most companies expect them to be certified in the product they use. A certification shows that the credential holder can design, implement, and manage the database in question. Some examples of common DBA certifications are Microsoft's Certified Database Administrator for SQL Server and the Oracle Database Administrator Certified Professional certification.

Volunteer Work and Internships

Database administration is an advanced profession, and database implementation and management is a long-term, time-intensive endeavor. For this reason, DBAs who volunteer their skills to assist nonprofits with database implementation or management are usually retired. However, internships are available for college students pursuing computer science and related degrees. Many technology companies offer internships to college students with the understanding that a successful internship may result in a job offer after graduation. For instance, Oracle has a summer paid internship program in product development that includes travel to and from school, paid housing, and car or bike rentals. The program is very competitive, but it offers valuable experiences to those who qualify. According to Oracle's product development internship website, an internship allows students to "get a foot in the door and perhaps even get the chance to interview early" for a position with the company upon graduation.

Skills and Personality

DBAs must have strong analytical and logical thinking skills. Their job entails visualizing complex relationships among data types, evaluating complex disparate information, and anticipating problems. Some of their tasks, such as performing backups and system tests, are repeated on a regular basis, so a DBA should not be adverse to methodical work. Most get satisfaction from organizing and enjoy paying close attention to details.

DBAs also interact with other workers on a regular basis. If they are employed by a small company, they may be required to assist their coworkers with system issues or run various data reports on request.

In larger companies, the DBA usually supervises several people and must have some management experience. They must also be able to communicate complex information to upper management and project stakeholders, many of whom may have little knowledge about databases and how they work.

On the Job

Employers

DBAs can work in almost any industry that collects and stores large amounts of data. The majority of DBAs work for companies that manage large amounts of data, such as hospitals, insurance companies, and large retailers. Internet marketing companies and data brokerage firms also rely on DBAs to manage their data. Some DBAs work for computer systems and services companies, such as Internet service providers and data processing companies.

Working Conditions

DBAs work indoors, and they often spend long hours at the computer working with code or data. The business environment depends on the company and its culture, but most DBAs work in a casual business environment. However, many DBAs are considered to be part of a company's management team, regardless of the number of people they supervise, and they may be subject to management's codes of dress and conduct.

Most DBAs work full time and often must be on-site after hours or on weekends to perform database operations with the least amount of disruption to other workers. According to the BLS, about 25 percent worked more than forty hours per week in 2012.

Earnings

The BLS found that the median annual wage for DBAs in 2012 was $77,080. The top 10 percent of DBAs earned more than $118,720, and the bottom 10 percent earned less than $42,930. Indeed.com lists the average salary of DBAs as $66,000 as of March 2014 and notes that their salaries are 14 percent higher than average salaries in the United States.

The salaries of DBAs depend on the industry in which they work. Top earners work in the finance and insurance industries, where DBAs can expect to earn a median salary of $85,880. The lowest-paid DBAs work in education and earn a median salary of $63,620.

Opportunities for Advancement

DBAs are often promoted to the position of computer and information system manager, which is also known as IT manager or IT project manager. IT managers are often in charge of all computer-related activities in an organization. They help management determine the organization's technology goals and then implement those goals. This is an upper-management position that paid a median salary of $120,950 in 2012.

The BLS lists four basic types of IT managers. IT directors, including management information systems directors, are directly in charge of a company's technology departments and their day-to-day workflow. IT security managers oversee network and data security. Chief technology officers design solutions and recommend options to top management. Finally, chief information officers are responsible for an organization's overall technology strategy. A talented DBA with business development experience can advance into these upper-management positions, especially if he or she has strong leadership skills.

What Is the Future Outlook for Database Administrators?

The BLS predicts that employment of DBAs is projected to grow 15 percent through 2022. This is slightly slower than the average growth predicted for computer occupations but faster than the average for all occupations. Companies in all sectors of the economy are predicted to have increased data needs, especially in health care, where use of electronic medical records is increasing. In general medical and surgical hospitals, employment of DBAs is expected to grow 43 percent. The cloud computing industry, in which data is managed off-site by a service provider, is also predicted to have an increased need for DBAs; the BLS predicts employment will grow by 48 percent. However, because new software tools are increasing the productivity of DBAs, growth in these two industries might be slightly slower than predicted.

Find Out More

Data Management International (DAMA)
phone: (813) 778-5495
website: www.dama.org

DAMA is a not-for-profit global association of technical and business professionals. Its website contains information about academic and training programs in data management, an extensive data resource management bibliography, and information about its Certified Data Management Professional (CDMP) certification program.

International DB2 Users Group (IDUG)
330 N. Wabash, Suite 2000
Chicago, IL 60611-4267
phone: (312) 321-6881
website: www.idug.org

An independent, not-for-profit organization, IDUG provides education and services to promote use of DB2, IBM's database server product. The organization holds industry conferences and technical seminars. Its website includes user forums, industry news and blogs, and a technical library that contains past seminars and journal articles. Some areas of the site are open only to members, but membership is free.

SearchDataManagement
website: http://searchdatamanagement.com

SearchDataManagement is a website that provides news, learning guides, expert advice, and webcasts to data management professionals. The site offers independent and vendor-produced content about various database management products. It also has a large archive of articles and podcasts of interest to IT professionals and those seeking a career in data management.

TDAN.com
PO Box 112571
Pittsburgh, PA 15241
phone: (412) 220-9643
website: www.tdan.com

TDAN.com is an online publication that contains articles and other resources for data management professionals and those considering a career in the industry. It also includes an archive of companies and products, books and book reviews, and event listings.

Computer Systems Analyst

What Does a Computer Systems Analyst Do?

Computer systems analysts design or redesign computer systems to meet an organization's business needs. They look at the big picture, asking questions such as: How will the system be used? Who are the users? What are the business objectives? How can the system stay within the budget? While systems analysts do not need to be experts in each component of a system, they must fully understand how hardware, software, and networks work together and the capacities and specifications of each. They must also understand business principles and be able to demonstrate a system's efficiency and return on investment to business executives within the company. Because systems analysts need such a unique skill set, they are in high demand. *U.S. News & World Report* named computer systems analyst as the number two job of 2014.

An entry-level systems analyst will usually be tasked with examining the specifications of a

---

At a Glance:

Computer Systems Analyst

Minimum Educational Requirements
Bachelor's degree

Personal Qualities
Creative thinking; strong analytical skills; strong interpersonal skills

Certification and Licensing
Optional

Working Conditions
Indoors

Salary Range
About $49,950 to $122,090

Number of Jobs
As of 2012 about 520 to 600

Future Job Outlook
Growth rate of 25 percent through 2022

single application under the supervision of a more experienced analyst. For instance, some junior analysts work within database programming, taking requests for alterations to the database system and determining how best to modify it. More advanced analysts manage entire projects. Some analysts choose to modify an existing retail system, and others build systems from scratch. They must consider a vast number of factors when making their design, such as whether a system will be on a shared drive in a network, on an intranet, or on the Internet; whether the system has enough capacity and memory to support heavy usage and accommodate future growth; what security is necessary; what types of data will be stored; what hardware and applications to purchase and how they will work together; and so forth. Those who supervise an installation or upgrade from start to finish are usually called IT project managers.

Most systems analysts specialize in specific environments (such as Unix) and in particular industries (such as financial), but many specialize further. Those who only work with organizations that are setting up or upgrading their computer systems are often called systems designers or systems architects. Experienced software testers who analyze the ways in which software works within a system are often known as software quality assurance analysts. They recommend ways in which the system, or the software, can be modified to improve efficiency or meet project goals. Software developers who design and update software that must work within a system in complex ways are often called programmer analysts. They do more coding and debugging than many traditional systems analysts—and often more than traditional software developers—but they also work closely with management to determine if business needs are being met.

How Do You Become a Computer Systems Analyst?

Education

Computer systems analysts must have a college degree. Most have a bachelor's degree in computer science, information technology, or another relevant field, but not always. It is becoming more and more common

41

for people with liberal arts degrees to switch careers and start working as systems analysts. According to career coach Marty Nemko, "Creative liberal-arts types with computer expertise usually make better systems analysts than pure techies." As he writes in *U.S. News & World Report*, "Being a systems analyst requires … the ability to see the big picture: translate geek-speak into plain English, identify company needs, and get everybody on board." People who have a math or science background can sometimes be very technical, which can hinder big-picture thinking.

Even if a systems analyst's undergraduate degree is in art or literature, he or she must still have gained significant knowledge and skills in computers. Systems analysts must have programming skills and broad knowledge of computer components, operating systems, networks, and so forth. Some must use statistics and math to solve problems; others must have a good grasp of how to apply engineering principles to design. Many analysts who come from a liberal arts or science background also have an interest in computers, and they have acquired this knowledge through self-study or elective classes.

Computer systems analysts must also have a background in business. For complex jobs, employers often like applicants to have a master's degree in business administration with a concentration in information systems. Sometimes applicants with highly technical skills can meet this requirement with a few electives in business systems analysis. Management information systems is another popular degree, since it combines business and technology. Those who plan to specialize in health care systems should take courses in health management or finance. And because the industry is constantly changing, all systems analysts should keep abreast of new technologies and continue their studies well past their formal education.

Certification

Computer systems analysts do not need any particular certifications, though entry-level systems analysts can earn an Information Systems Analyst certification from the Institute for the Certification of Computing Professionals. The institute also offers advanced certifications, which can serve to set an applicant apart in the job market. Other certifications may or may not help a job seeker—it depends on the hiring company's specific needs.

Volunteer Work and Internships

There are few volunteer opportunities for computer systems analysts who are not retired, because the process is time-consuming. However, many students become interested in systems analysis because they have helped friends, family members, or even nonprofits choose computers systems or have built them systems from scratch. This sort of experience can lead to a valuable internship during high school or college.

Internships are available with computer systems design firms as well as large technology companies. For instance, Intel has a robust internship program for both undergraduate and graduate students with opportunities to learn about systems analysis by working on ongoing projects for clients. Students must have a good grade point average and some advanced experience in the project's focus. For instance, a systems analysis project dealing with Big Data would require experience in SQL querying and data modeling—or at least a strong interest in these areas. Successful completion of an internship will usually lead to a job offer after graduation.

Skills and Personality

Computer systems analysts need to be independent, creative thinkers. They must be able to come up with innovative solutions for complex problems, grasp highly technical concepts quickly, and see the big picture without getting bogged down in the details. They also need to be able to develop many ideas at a time while still seeing how each part fits into the whole. People who naturally have this unique blend of logical and creative thinking skills will thrive as systems analysts.

Strong interpersonal skills are also important. Analysts must be able to communicate with business leaders, technology experts, and end users. They must be good listeners who can find a way to meet the needs of each of these diverse groups. They also often work in a team environment, so they need to be able to work well with others. Many systems analysts also supervise junior programmers or other team members, so good management skills are helpful. Finally, analysts are often called on to make presentations to a project's stakeholders, so they must be able to convey complex ideas clearly, both during a presentation and in written documentation.

On the Job

Employers

About a quarter of all computer systems analysts work for computer systems design firms. The rest work in a diverse range of industries, including science, health care, banking and finance, education, and government. Government agencies and universities, which historically are very stable places to work, are also some of the top employers of systems analysts. More and more private sector companies are hiring systems analysts on a temporary or contract basis to complete a specific project. Because of this, many systems analysts work as consultants for IT firms that offer computer systems solutions to organizations seeking to upgrade their systems.

Working Conditions

Computer systems analysts work indoors, usually in a business or business casual environment. Most work full time with occasional overtime; however, when a new system first goes online, analysts can expect to be on call twenty-four hours a day. In 2012 about 25 percent of all systems analysts worked more than forty hours per week. Some analysts can telecommute at certain times during a project, but they must be on the job site at least part of the time to evaluate current systems, meet with management, and perform installations and testing.

Earnings

The BLS found that the median annual wage for computer systems analysis in 2012 was $79,680. The top 10 percent of all analysts earned more than $122,090, and the bottom 10 percent earned less than $49,950. Computer systems analysts earned slightly more than the average of all other computer occupations, and more than twice as much as the average for all other occupations. Some of the highest-paid positions are in the mining industry and in the securities and commodities exchanges. The highest-paying jobs are along the East Coast of the United States. The highest-paying cities are Bridgeport, Connecticut, where analysts make an average of $116,560 per year; and Sarasota, Florida, and State College, Pennsylvania, where analysts make an average of about $109,000 per year.

Opportunities for Advancement

As computer systems analysts gain experience, they progress to more senior positions, with higher pay and more responsibility. They frequently become IT project managers and are responsible for every phase of the project, from development to maintenance. After accumulating about ten years of experience, most systems analysts are qualified to run a company's technology department as their chief technical/technology officer (CTO). These technology professionals can earn very high salaries and bonuses, depending on the industry. Talented systems analysts who join start-ups can find themselves in a CTO position more quickly, though they are also likely to be laid off if the company fails. Independent consultants with ten or more years' experience earn in excess of $125 per hour.

What Is the Future Outlook for Computer Systems Analysts?

According to the BLS, the job market for computer systems analysts is predicted to grow 25 percent through 2022, faster than the average of all other computer occupations. The BLS predicts that part of this increase will be due to growth in cloud computing and wireless and mobile networks, which will create a need for new or redesigned computer systems that will be able to work with this new technology. Health care is another field that will see an increase in systems analyst hiring. As more hospitals embrace electronic medical records and e-prescribing, analysts will need to redesign systems to accommodate these new technological changes.

Computer systems design firms will see the biggest increase in hiring of systems analysts. These firms will see an increase in business from small- and medium-sized organizations that need advanced computer systems. Computer systems design firms usually employ consultants, who move from project to project. Employment of systems analysts in these firms is predicted to grow 35 percent through 2022.

Find Out More

International Institute of Business Analysis (IIBA)
701 Rossland Road East, Suite 356
Whitby, ON L1N 9K3
Canada
phone: (866) 789-4422
website: www.iiba.org

The IIBA is an independent nonprofit professional association serving the growing field of business and systems analysis. The IIBA's website has a section devoted to learning and development that includes an online library, webinars, and vendor showcase videos. It also has a career guide for business and systems analysts.

League of Professional System Administrators (LOPSA)
PO Box 5161
Trenton, NJ 08638
phone: (202) 567-7201
website: http://lopsa.org

LOPSA is a nonprofit corporation that advances the practice of system administration and analysis by supporting, recognizing, and educating its practitioners. Its website has information about its mentorship program, which connects students with those more experienced in the field.

Robert Half Technology
website: www.roberthalf.com

Robert Half Technology is an IT consulting company that employs IT professionals in various fields. Its website has dozens of in-depth articles that discuss the job challenges faced by systems analysts.

USENIX: The Advanced Computing Systems Association
2560 Ninth Street, Suite 215
Berkeley, CA 94710
phone: (510) 528-8649
website: www.usenix.org

With more than seven thousand members, the Advanced Computing Systems Association brings together engineers, system administrators, scientists, and technicians working in the computing field. USENIX offers grants and awards to students and has a USENIX campus representative program that provides information to students.

Information Security Analyst

What Does an Information Security Analyst Do?

Cybercrime—which can be defined as any crime that involves a computer and a network—is on the rise. According to a survey sponsored by Hewlett-Packard, cybercrime went up in 2013 for the fourth consecutive year, rising 26 percent between 2012 and 2013. The survey revealed that the cyberattacks are getting more sophisticated and costly, and companies are beefing up their security with advanced security tools. Spending on information security is expected to be $86 billion in 2016—almost a $20 billion increase over spending in 2013.

The first line of defense against cybercrime is the information security analyst. Information security analysts are responsible for protecting computer networks and the data they contain. They have three main areas of focus: risk assessment, vulnerability assessment, and defense planning. Risk assess-

At a Glance:

Information Security Analyst

Minimum Educational Requirements
Bachelor's degree

Personal Qualities
Strong analytical and problem-solving skills; ingenuity; high tolerance for stress

Certification and Licensing
Strongly suggested

Working Conditions
Indoors

Salary Range
About $49,960 to $135,600

Number of Jobs
As of 2012 about 75,100

Future Job Outlook
Growth rate of 37 percent through 2022

ment entails identifying the types of problems an organization might face, such as computer viruses, cyberattacks, and so forth. Vulnerability assessment entails identifying the potential weak spots in a network or a security protocol that a cyberattacker might exploit, such as a back door, or open access point, that was used in a prior project and then forgotten. And defense planning involves installing countermeasures to these threats, such as encryption programs and firewalls. Information security analysts also must constantly reevaluate these countermeasures and weigh their effectiveness against the current threat climate.

Information security analysts must have advanced knowledge of their organization's computer system—often as much as the computer systems analyst or chief technology officer. On a typical day, a security analyst will conduct research on the latest security issues pertaining to the software and systems in use, download and install any system patches issued by software manufacturers, and send out alerts about any suspicious e-mail scams or viruses that are in circulation. He or she will also prepare documentation, including department policies and procedures and training materials, and meet with management to discuss security vulnerabilities or initiatives. Junior-level analysts may be responsible for operating the software that analyzes and monitors the network for security breaches, or they may conduct staff training on new security procedures. Senior-level analysts are responsible for conducting investigative work when a security breach has occurred. The process of investigating cybercrime is known as computer or digital forensics, which has the goal of identifying, preserving, recovering, and analyzing evidence around an instance of cybercrime. Digital forensics is an advanced field of information security, but information security analysts often have to employ forensic investigative techniques to get to the bottom of a data breach and determine if it resulted from a cyberattack.

How Do You Become an Information Security Analyst?

Education

An information security analyst must have a bachelor's degree, usually in computer science, management information systems, or a related field. In response to the increased need for trained information security analysts, some schools are providing information security training programs, though the BLS notes that "currently, a well-rounded computer education is preferred." Most security analysts have several years' experience in a related occupation; some have a background in network or system administration, and others are database programmers or administrators. Many employers prefer security analysts to have a master's degree in business information with a concentration in information systems.

In addition, information security analysts must continue to acquire skills in their field and keep informed about the security risks inherent in the latest technologies, such as wireless networks and cloud computing. They must also be familiar with security regulations and standards that apply to their industry. For instance, security analysts working in retail must know the Payment Card Industry Data Security Standard, which pertains to the prevention and detection of credit card security incidents. They must also love learning about security. According to Matthew Fuller, a recent graduate with a focus in computer security, "A career in security is not one that can be performed at the office and separated from the rest of your life. To be successful, you need to be involved in the industry, reading blogs by security researchers, and even doing research yourself."

Certification

Most employers require information security analysts to be certified in the products they will be working with, as well as to hold general certifications. The Certified Information Systems Security Professional (CISSP) certification is a vendor-neutral credential offered by the International Information Systems Security Certification Consortium. To earn the CISSP, applicants must have five years of related work experience, pass the exam, and be endorsed by an active member of the organization. Recertification is required every three years, as are continuing education credits, which can be earned through publishing, attending conferences, or providing training to others. The exam fee is between $500 and $600, with an annual maintenance fee of $85. The Global Information Assurance Certification is another general certification that has similar requirements.

Volunteer Work and Internships

Information security analysts rarely perform volunteer work, though some retired analysts provide mentoring services to nonprofits. There are, however, many opportunities for undergraduate and graduate students to gain experience through internships. For instance, the US Department of Homeland Security has a Cybersecurity Internship Program. According to the department's website, "Internships focus on mission areas such as identification and analysis of malicious code, forensics analysis, incident handling, intrusion detection and prevention, and software assurance." The National Security Agency and the Federal Bureau of Investigation also have internship programs in various disciplines, including cybersecurity. Also, according to Fuller, many companies are "extremely willing" to take interns into their security departments. He suggests that college freshmen with an interest in security "jump at internships opportunities the first chance you get. If you have no plans [for an internship] for the summer after freshman year, you are likely going to be behind."

Skills and Personality

Information security analysts must have strong analytical and problem-solving skills. They also should have a certain amount of ingenuity; they must be able to anticipate and prepare for security problems before they occur and be able to act quickly and effectively when they do. Security analysts must also be detail oriented, patient, and observant to be able to catch minor changes in system performance that might indicate a security breach.

Information security analysts must also be able to handle stress. When a cyberattack happens, security analysts must focus on the task at hand to identify how the breach occurred and secure the system. This can be difficult when the organization is in panic mode, especially if the security team is viewed as being at fault. It can also be stressful to be on call during off-hours, which some can find disruptive to family life.

On the Job

Employers

About a quarter of all information security analysts work for computer systems design firms. The rest work in a diverse range of industries, including finance and insurance, information, and enterprise management (companies that specialize in monitoring and interpreting computerized business activities). Because of the sensitive nature of their work, very few security analysts are self-employed.

Working Conditions

Computer systems analysts work indoors, usually in a casual environment. Most work full time. They also can be on call after hours in case of a security emergency.

Earnings

The BLS found that the median annual wage for computer systems analysis in 2012 was $86,170. The top 10 percent of all analysts earned more than $135,600, and the bottom 10 percent earned less than $49,960. Computer systems analysts earned more than the average of all other computer occupations, and more than twice as much as the average of all other occupations. Indeed.com found that the average salary of information security analysts as of April 2014 was $69,000. Some of the highest-paid positions are in the finance and insurance industries, though health care and government also pay well. The highest-paying jobs are in California and the Northeast.

Opportunities for Advancement

Information security analysts can move into senior positions and advance to chief security officer. Some information security analysts become chief technology officers of their companies. Information security analysts who wish to specialize can work in many exciting areas related to computer crime and cybersecurity. The computer security training institute SANS lists information security crime investigator/forensic expert as number one on its list of the "20 Coolest Jobs in Information Security." These experts specialize in investigating computer crime while preserving the evidence so that the criminals can be prosecuted. Number two on the list is system, network, and/or web penetration tester. These specialists, sometimes called "pen testers," are essentially professional hackers who probe systems for vulnerabilities. According to security expert Ed Skoudis, "The power to understand how systems can be penetrated and misused is something less than one percent of people in the entire security industry know, let alone the average citizen."

What Is the Future Outlook for Information Security Analysts?

U.S. News & World Report ranked information security analyst fourth on its list of the best technology jobs of 2014. One reason for this is that employment of information security analysts is expected to rise a whopping 37 percent through 2022, according to the BLS. Growth in this industry may be due to the high-profile security breaches that have happened in the past several years. One of the largest was the December 2013 data breach of 110 million Target customer records, which included credit and debit card information. Security analysts working at Target did not realize the breach had occurred until the US Department of Justice brought it to their attention three weeks later. According to a March 2014 article in *Bloomberg Businessweek*, the malware used in the cyberattack was not especially sophisticated, and Target was protected by a monitoring service, which alerted the retailer that the malware had been installed. However, Target's security team overlooked the alert. According to a Verizon study, only 5 percent of retailers discover security breaches through their own monitoring efforts—most likely because security is not a retailer's focus. The scope of the Target breach has now made information security a priority for all businesses that store sensitive information.

According to the BLS, the US government is also expected to increase its use of information security analysts to protect critical IT systems, which are vulnerable to cyberattacks from terrorists and foreign powers. The health care industry is also expected to hire more information security analysts to support its increasing use of electronic health records.

Find Out More

Computer Forensics World
website: http://computerforensicsworld.com

Computer Forensics World is a community of professionals involved in the digital forensics industry. It is open resource and free for all to access and use. Its website includes forums, posting areas, and educational materials on computer forensics and security.

Information Systems Security Association (ISSA)
9220 SW Barbur Blvd., #119-333
Portland, OR 97219
phone: (866) 349-5818
website: www.issa.org

The ISSA is a not-for-profit, international organization of information security professionals and practitioners. It provides educational forums, publications, and peer interaction opportunities that enhance the knowledge, skill, and professional growth of its members.

National Security Institute (NSI)
165 Main St., Suite 215
Medway, MA 02053
phone: (508) 533-9099
website: www.nsi.org

The NSI is dedicated to helping companies and governmental agencies understand threats to security. Its information services are used by top corporations to educate employees about risks to critical information from hackers, spies, and data thieves. The NSI's website contains articles and special reports about computer security.

SANS Institute
8120 Woodmont Ave., Suite 205
Bethesda, MD 20814
phone: (301) 654-7267
website: www.sans.org

The SANS Institute is a cooperative research and education organization that provides information security training and security certification. It develops, maintains, and makes available at no cost the largest collection of research documents about various aspects of information security.

Wireless Network Architect

Businesses that have multiple computers usually connect them together in what is called a local area network (LAN) so that the computers can share data, applications, and storage space. In a traditional network, computers are connected to each other and to the Internet with a series of cables. Wireless networks (also known as Wi-Fi networks or WLAN) do away with these cables, transmitting and receiving data over electromagnetic waves. While consumers can usually set up small networks themselves, when a larger business goes wireless it needs the services of a wireless network architect.

A wireless network architect designs, installs, and troubleshoots wireless computer networks. These computer professionals have specialized knowledge about electromagnetic wave frequencies and how different materials will conduct or block a wireless signal. There

At a Glance:

Wireless Network Architect

Minimum Educational Requirements
Bachelor's degree

Personal Qualities
Creative problem solving; detail oriented; strong interpersonal skills

Certification and Licensing
Strongly suggested

Working Conditions
Mostly indoors

Salary Range
About $33,500 to $105,200

Number of Jobs
As of 2012 about 143,400 (includes traditional and wireless network architects)

Future Job Outlook
Growth rate of 15 percent through 2022*

*Includes traditional and wireless network architects.

are thousands of variables that affect the signal strength. For instance, a wireless architect knows that the leaves on a tree diffuse wireless signals far more than a concrete wall, that it is harder for a signal to pass through drywall in a humid climate than in a dry climate, and that certain colors of paint affect a signal in different ways. Architects must also know what variables will change in the future. If a neighboring building installs Wi-Fi, if there is new construction in the area, or even if the business is planning to get new furniture in six months, the wireless network will be affected. As wireless expert David Hucaby writes in a 2013 article for Cisco Press, "Wireless networking is so full of variables that I'm often amazed that it even works!"

Along with vast technical knowledge about computer networking and electromagnetic frequencies, a wireless network architect must have strong interpersonal and communication skills. Most of the information the architect needs comes from extensive consultations with the business owner, who may not understand the complexities of wireless technology. These business owners may inadvertently withhold crucial information because they underestimate their needs or because they do not want to reveal sensitive information about future plans. It is crucial that architects establish trust and rapport with their clients; otherwise they run the risk of designing a network based on incomplete information.

A typical installation project begins with the architect spending many hours mapping and surveying the coverage area and asking questions to determine where to place the wireless access points. The architect then calculates coverage areas using algebra, geometry, and knowledge of the conductivity of the various materials the signal will pass through. However, what works on paper rarely works in the real world, and architects must also draw on past experiences and intuition. This is why many in the industry say wireless networking is both a science and an art form.

Wireless architects must also be knowledgeable about how to test their networks, track down interference, calibrate equipment, provide network security, and make sure that a variety of mobile devices coexist on the network. Architects must also keep abreast of new technologies so that they can design systems today that can integrate those technologies tomorrow. According to Wil Ankerstjerne, a leader in the wireless network solutions industry, "Wireless is endlessly challenging. You never run out of things to learn."

How Do You Become a Wireless Network Architect?

Education

Wireless network architects must have an intuitive grasp of mathematics, chemistry, physics, and earth sciences. They know a great deal about computer systems and networks and have specialized knowledge about the behavior of electromagnetic waves. To prepare for a career in wireless networking, high school students should take advanced science, math, and computer science courses.

Wireless network architects usually have a bachelor's degree in the sciences—frequently computer science or computer engineering—and they supplement their knowledge with training programs, certifications, and self-study. Some are required to have a master's degree in computer science or business administration. However, because wireless is a relatively new technology that is constantly changing, only so much can be learned in the classroom. Architects must have plenty of hands-on experience and must be willing to learn on the job. It is possible for an individual to work as a wireless network architect with only an associate's degree; however, these individuals are rare. They must have ample experience and the necessary certifications.

Most architects spend a few years as installers or administrators in traditional networks and then a few years working with wireless technology before they have enough knowledge to design a network. Others are computer systems analysts or architects or engineers of traditional computer networks who have decided to shift their career focus to wireless technology.

Certification

Various certifications are available in the wireless industry. Certifications are voluntary, but it is difficult to secure a job in networking without any certifications. Some demonstrate general knowledge about the technology, such as the Certified Wireless Networking Professional, which is available in entry through expert level. Other certifications are in specific wireless technologies, which are constantly being developed. Many companies require certification for wireless network installers and administrators. Architects usually must have up-to-date certifications in all current technologies. Some companies require architects to take the Cisco Certified Architect Board Exam, which costs about $15,000. It is offered by Cisco Systems, a company that sells computer networking equipment. Microsoft also offers an architect-level networking certification.

Internships and Mentoring

Internships are occasionally available for college students interested in wireless networking design, but students are more likely to find internships in general computer network administration and system design—often in the IT department of a large company. These types of internships are still valuable, since architects must have extensive knowledge of computer systems, system administration, and networking principles. Any internship that gives a student experience with computer systems is an important first step toward working with wireless technology.

Since so much of wireless networking is learned on the job, informal mentoring is also quite common in this industry. Those interested in the technology should seek out experienced architects and try to learn all they can from them. Mentors can also help guide those new to the industry toward jobs that will provide crucial experience.

Skills and Personality

A wireless network architect has to love the challenge of solving problems in innovative ways. Nothing is black and white in the wireless industry, and those looking for predictable outcomes will not find them. "You have to love the technology and love the challenge," explains Ankerstjerne. "Those who don't will find it endlessly frustrating."

Wireless architects typically have a natural aptitude in IT and mathematics, as well as an interest in chemistry, physics, and earth science. They enjoy bringing all of their knowledge to bear when solving a problem and are always interested in innovative solutions. Because architects usually work with a team, they must enjoy collaborative work.

Architects also must have strong interpersonal and customer-relations skills. They need to be able to form a partnership with their clients so that they can get the information necessary to design an effective system. They also must be able to document their work, so strong written communication skills are also necessary.

Employers

Wireless network architects are often hired by wireless solution companies—businesses that both sell and install wireless hardware. Some architects are hired full time and move from project to project. Others are hired on a temporary basis as contract workers for specific projects. A company that has already transitioned to a wireless network will sometimes hire a wireless network architect to administer and troubleshoot its network. However, unless a company is very large or has complex needs, a wireless network administrator can handle routine maintenance. Hospitals are likely to hire architects in permanent positions because of the complexity of their networks.

Working Conditions

Wireless network architects spend a lot of time on their feet when surveying a site. Some industry insiders joke that wireless professionals are never at their desks; they spend most of their days roaming the hallways and staring at the ceiling. Sometimes they must survey crawl spaces, ductwork, basements, and building exteriors. The rest of their time is spent designing networks on the computer, calibrating and installing equipment, and meeting with clients. Architects usually have to travel to the job site each day, and many work far from home and live in hotels for the duration of a project. Those who find permanent positions spend a great deal of time interacting with employees and troubleshooting coverage issues.

Wireless network architects usually work full time. More than 25 percent of all computer network architects (including architects of traditional networks) work more than forty hours a week. Architects typically must meet project deadlines, which can entail long hours.

Earnings

Most earnings reports for wireless network architects group the position in with traditional computer network architects. The BLS found that the median annual wage for all computer network architects in 2012 was $91,000. The top 10 percent earned more than $141,590, and the bottom 10 percent earned less than $52,580. A Robert Half Technology survey found that the starting salary of all computer network architects (including wireless) in 2013 was $102,250 to $146,500, a 7.3 percent increase over 2012.

Simply Hired lists the average salary of wireless network architects as $93,000 as of March 2014. Indeed.com lists the average salary as $108,000 as of March 2014 and notes that their salaries are 48 percent higher than average salaries in the United States.

Opportunities for Advancement

Wireless network architect is the highest designation in wireless networking. The best architects are hired to work on projects for high-profile, complex organizations. Skilled architects who also have strong interpersonal and managerial skills are often promoted to project management or technical director positions.

What Is the Future Outlook for Wireless Network Architects?

Many technology experts predict that all computer networks will be wireless in the future. The speed, capacity, and security of wireless networks already rival traditional computer networks, and many people already have wireless networks in their homes. A 2013 survey by AT&T found that 98 percent of small businesses use wireless networks, and more and more large companies are going wireless every year. Because wireless networks untether employees from their workstations, they are extremely valuable to hospitals, universities, airports, or any organization where people regularly work away from their desks. Hospitals in particular are relying more and more on mobile devices, which operate over wireless networks.

The BLS predicts that employment of all computer network architects will grow by 15 percent through 2022. This increase is due to growth in the use of wireless networks, so most of these new jobs will be in wireless network architecture. In addition, industry leaders predict that more innovative mobile devices will hit the market in the coming years, which increases the need for wireless network architects. A 2013 *Computerworld* Forecast survey of 221 IT executives found that 31 percent intended to hire individuals with networking skills. Scot Melland, CEO of the company that owns the IT jobs website Dice.com, told *Computerworld* in 2013 that "demand for people with wireless networking experience is up nine percent year after year" and the unemployment rate among networking professionals is 1.1 percent, which he attributes to the need of companies to have wireless connectivity.

Find Out More

International Association for Radio, Telecommunications and Electromagnetics (iNARTE)
600 N. Plankinton Ave., Suite 301
Milwaukee, WI 53201
phone: (888) 722-2440
website: http://narte.org

iNARTE is a nonprofit membership/certification organization that provides a comprehensive certification program for telecommunications engineers and technicians. Its website has information about the Wireless Device Certification Professional certification and has links to study materials.

International Association of Engineers (IAENG):
Society of Wireless Networks
website: http://iaeng.org

Through regularly scheduled conferences and workshops on wireless networks, the IAENG Society of Wireless Networks serves as a forum for networking, information sharing, idea exchange, and problem solving for the wireless network community. Its website contains links to news and publications about wireless networking.

Wireless Design and Development
199 E. Badger Rd., Suite 101
Madison, WI 53713
website: www.wirelessdesignmag.com

Wireless Design and Development is a free online magazine that provides educational resources to wireless engineers working with radio frequencies and microwaves. Issues contain articles by industry professionals and introductions to new products and technology. Many educational resources are also available.

Wireless Technology Forum
6300 Powers Ferry Rd., Suite 600-140
Atlanta, GA 30339
website: http://wirelesstechnologyforum.org

The Wireless Technology Forum is a nonprofit association that provides a venue for wireless professionals to learn about the business of emerging wireless and mobile technologies, network with other like-minded professionals, and apply these technologies to their existing business or creation of a new business.

Software Developer

What Does a Software Developer Do?

Software developers (also known as software engineers) are the creative experts who plan, design, and build computer programs. According to experts, software developers are in high demand, and those who enter this field are well paid and rarely unemployed. Both *Forbes* and *U.S. News & World Report* named software developer as the number one job of 2014. Nearly every company in the IT industry employs software developers in one capacity or another, and that need is growing. According to Matt Ferguson, CEO of CareerBuilder, "Companies want to go to market first with innovations; they want to extract, parse and apply Big Data to make smarter business decisions and create better solutions for clients. Software developers play a key role in these initiatives."

There are two primary types of software developers: application developers and systems developers. Application developers create the programs that run on computers or other devices. The popular mobile app *Angry Birds*, the word processing program Microsoft Word, and the web browser Firefox are all examples of computer applications designed by software

At a Glance:
Software Developer

Minimum Educational Requirements
Bachelor's degree

Personal Qualities
Creativity; detail oriented; strong interpersonal skills

Certification and Licensing
Strongly suggested

Working Conditions
Indoors

Salary Range
About $55,190 to $138,880

Number of Jobs
As of 2012 about 1 million

Future Job Outlook
Growth rate of 22 percent through 2022

application developers. Some application developers are hired by organizations to custom design software to fit their needs. Others develop applications designed to run on the Internet. The health care marketplace portal HealthCare.gov is an example of a web-based application designed—and then redesigned—by a team of software application developers.

Systems developers create the software that operates a computer's hardware. Microsoft Windows, Linux, and Mac OS X are examples of operating systems created by software systems developers. These operating systems allow computer applications to interface with the computer's hardware. Systems developers also create unique software that allows users to interface with other types of devices that use computers. The computers in modern cars, which power everything from the air-conditioning to the antilock brakes, are designed by systems software developers.

Software developers typically work in teams. Software development is a highly structured process. Entry-level developers usually work in only one facet of development, whereas lead software developers are involved in all stages. Lead developers work with the clients or stakeholders to understand everything from the function of the software to the desired appearance and user interface. They oversee the team that designs each part of the software and determine how all parts will work together. They also create detailed instructions for graphic artists and programmers to create various components of the application or system and thoroughly test their final product, often with the assistance of software testers. One lead software developer told the *Princeton Review* that she saw herself as a chef: "The parts I have to put together are the ingredients, and I have to decide how and when to put them together to make a beautiful dish."

Although software developers frequently work in teams, some work alone, designing software and writing code themselves. Some of the most popular software applications were created by software developers working alone or with a partner. For instance, the online photo-sharing application Snapchat was created in 2011 by two Stanford University fraternity brothers when they were twenty-three and twenty-five years old. And the mobile game *Flappy Bird*, which was the most downloaded free game in the Apple App Store in January

2014, was created by twenty-eight-year-old computer programmer Dong Nguyen in his spare time. These solo developers often make the news because of their youth, but most of them have been programming computers since they were teenagers and have a decade or more of experience under their belts.

Although application developers and systems developers are the two major types of software developers, there is often specialization within each type. Some software developers specialize in certain industries, such as aerospace, business, or health care. Many software developers in the health care industry specialize in creating user interfaces for complex databases, such as those used in electronic health record systems in doctors' offices and hospitals. Other software developers specialize in mobile applications, system software for innovative devices, computer-generated animation software, search engine software, and even computer games like *World of Warcraft*. Game designers in particular draw upon a wide variety of skills. They not only need to have high-level software development and programming abilities, they need to have expert understanding of computer animation, the gaming platform they are working with, and user interface and gaming psychology.

How Do You Become a Software Developer?

Education

Most software developers—about 75 percent—have a bachelor's degree. Only about 7 percent have an associate's degree, and 17 percent have a master's degree. Software developers usually pursue a degree in computer science, computer engineering, or software engineering, though some are math majors who minor in computer science. All software developers must know several programming languages, and many start as programmers. Others come to software engineering from other disciplines. Even though most software developers have degrees in computer science, developers are usually hired based on their track record. The software that a developer has created is an important part of a job seeker's résumé.

In the United States there is a shortage of skilled software developers. Not enough students are taking computer science classes in high school or pursing computer science in college to fill the growing need for developers in the job market. High school students who pursue this field are all but guaranteed employment after graduating from college.

Certification

Most software developers hold multiple certifications. Certifications are available in a wide variety of applications, such as database management system software (such as MySQL), development software (such as Visual Basic and Python), and web platform development software (such as ColdFusion). The type of certification necessary depends on industry trends and the preferences of individual employers. Some employers pay for certifications, but others expect employees to foot the bill.

Volunteer Work and Internships

Although there are few volunteer opportunities for entry-level software developers, internships are very common. They are frequently offered to computer science majors by companies both large and small that are looking for new talent, and many interns are offered permanent positions upon graduation. Internships are also available to talented high school students who plan to pursue software development as a career.

Skills and Personality

Software developers must have a wide variety of skills, from complex problem solving to critical thinking. Most must know a great deal about computer systems and networks to determine how software will interact with these platforms. Nearly all developers are fluent in several computer programming languages and can be extremely detail oriented when the task demands it. Software developers also need strong math skills.

Since many software developers are involved in multiple stages of development, they must have excellent interpersonal and communication skills. They must understand the needs of their clients or stakeholders and effectively bridge the gap between those stakeholders and members of their teams. Software developers who manage entire projects must coordinate all tasks and team communication. Developers of all levels also have the task of documenting their work, so strong written communication skills are also necessary.

On the Job

Employers

Software developers work for a variety of companies. Some are contractors or work for software solutions companies. These developers move from project to project, often relocating every few years. Other developers are hired directly by companies that need specialized software developed, such as online retailers like Amazon, or by companies that create software products, such as Internet security companies like Norton. Other developers work with manufacturers to develop specialized system software for electronic devices. About a third of all software developers design software systems; the remainder are applications developers. Still other software developers work independently, creating applications on their own or in small teams.

Working Conditions

Software developers work indoors, often in a casual environment. Many work in teams and must meet frequently with graphic designers, programmers, and marketing professionals. Most work full time and often must work long hours to meet project deadlines; according to the BLS, more than 25 percent worked more than forty hours per week in 2012. Some software developers telecommute at least a few days a week.

Earnings

The BLS found that the median annual wage for all software developers in 2012 was $93,350. Systems developers earned slightly more than application developers, with a median wage of $99,000 versus $90,060. The top 10 percent of all developers earned more than $138,880, and the bottom 10 percent earned less than $55,190. A 2013 Robert Half Technology survey found that the starting salary for mobile application software developers was $92,750 to $133,500, a 9 percent increase over 2012. Indeed.com lists the average salary of software developers

During a hackathon, software developers collaborate in the creation of new, usable software products. Software developers (or engineers) plan, design, and build computer programs. They are well paid and in high demand.

as $91,000 as of March 2014 and notes that their salaries are 54 percent higher than average salaries in the United States.

The news is filled with accounts of independent software developers writing applications that become instant hits. Many of these applications are web based, and developers are paid either through advertising revenue or by their software being acquired by larger companies. Most software developers who go this route have fulltime jobs and make very little from their ventures, but some become overnight successes. For instance, the creator of the mobile app *Flappy Bird* was earning $50,000 a day in ad revenue before he removed the game for personal reasons, and in 2013, Facebook offered the creators of Snapchat $3 billion dollars for the messaging app (the young developers declined the offer).

Opportunities for Advancement

Software developers earn higher salaries and are given more responsibility as they gain experience. Developers progress to senior or lead positions, and some become software architects. Though the title is not well defined, software architects typically focus on the analysis and design of large, complex projects. Software developers with very strong interpersonal and managerial skills are often promoted to project management. Other developers move into specializations that require more advanced skills, such as game design or computer security.

What Is the Future Outlook for Software Developers?

The employment prospects for computer science and software development graduates is excellent. According to technology expert Bryan Cantrill, software developers are in "absolutely explosive demand." He tells *U.S. News & World Report*, "We're seeing a gap between the number of software engineers we need and the number the education system is generating. . . . This is a terrific area to invest oneself." The BLS predicts that employment of software developers will grow by 22 percent through 2022. The reason for this growth is an increased need for computer software, especially in the health care and mobile applications industries, combined with a projected shortfall in computer science graduates. For this reason, the unemployment rate for software developers is predicted to be between 1 and 3 percent, well below the national average.

Find Out More

Association for Computer Machinery (ACM)
2 Penn Pl., Suite 701
New York, NY 10121
phone: (800) 342-6626
website: www.acm.org

The ACM is the premier membership organization for computing professionals. It hosts the computing industry's Digital Library and sponsors journals and magazines, conferences, workshops, and electronic forums. The ACM has many resources for students, including scholarship opportunities.

Association for Women in Computing (AWC)
PO Box 2768
Oakland, CA 94602
e-mail: info@awc-hq.org
website: www.awc-hq.org

The AWC is one of the first professional organizations for women in computing. The AWC is dedicated to promoting the advancement of women in the computing professions and providing opportunities for professional growth through networking and through programs on technical and career-oriented topics.

Association of Software Professionals (ASP)
PO Box 1522
Martinsville, IN 46151
phone: (765) 349-4740
website: http://asp-software.org

The ASP is a professional trade association of software developers who are creating and marketing leading-edge applications. Members and vendors can share their experiences with software development in an online forum environment. The organization also publishes in-depth business and marketing articles in its monthly newsletter.

Software Engineering Institute (SEI)
4500 Fifth Ave.
Pittsburgh, PA 15213
phone: (888) 201-4479
website: www.sei.cmu.edu

The SEI is a federally funded research and development center, founded in 1984 and sponsored by the US Department of Defense with the core purpose of helping others make measured improvements in their software engineering capabilities. The SEI's website contains many resources, including a digital library and archived podcasts and webinars.

Interview with a Wireless Network Architect

Wil Ankerstjerne is a senior wireless solutions architect for Aspire Technology Partners in New Jersey. He has more than fifteen years of wireless technology consulting experience and has managed more than 250 wireless projects, including Children's Hospital of Philadelphia and Panera Bread. Ankerstjerne has been a keynote speaker at several high-profile industry events and recently conducted a webinar for Fluke Networks on the latest wireless networking standard. He spoke with the author about his career.

Q: Why did you become a wireless network architect?

A: I got a break during the Y2K crisis [the concern that computer systems that stored year values as two digits (e.g., 99 for 1999) would malfunction on January 1, 2000] and was hired as a project manager for an IT solutions firm. I was doing a lot of traditional network installations, but after a while it wasn't very challenging. When you have a wired network, the main problem you run into is how to run a cable from point A to point B. But a wireless signal can be affected by anything and everything. When I discovered how cool wireless could be, I shifted my focus.

Q: Can you describe your typical workday?

A: I spend a lot of time walking around with floor plans and doing calculations, and then factoring in all of the elements in the environment that the calculations just can't account for—like the density of the furniture or the moisture in the air. Essentially, I'm making a string of educated guesses about how many access points we need and where they should go. I'm also anticipating future changes in technology as well as unpredictable stuff that could affect the signal, like whether or not a company is going to move in upstairs, or whether they're going to get all new furniture, or use a particular kind of paint. Then I have to write it all up in a way that will convince the client that, yes, you really do need thirty-two hundred access points, and here's why.

Q: What do you like most and least about your job?

A: I love the challenge. On every single project, I have to use my brain outside of the box. Nothing works the same way twice. I'm always trying something new, and I'm always learning something. I can work with somebody who's been out of school for less than six months and learn something new because they picked up on something on their last job or had an instructor who knew something I didn't know.

Hands down what I like least about my job is the documentation. A customer will say to me, "At home I can cover five thousand square feet with one access point, so why do I need thirty access points to cover the thirty thousand square feet in my office?" I have to justify my design to them by proving the coverage and performance of a wireless network that doesn't exist yet. This paperwork can be quite daunting, because you have to describe the way an invisible technology works to someone who doesn't have any technical knowledge, and you can't just show them the math because, nine times out of ten, the math doesn't work in the real world.

Q: What personal qualities do you find most valuable for this type of work?

A: The most valuable thing is interpersonal skill. My customers become my friends. They really have to, because I'm "selling" them an invisible product that they don't understand. And I'm telling them that I have looked into my magic ball and foreseen how things will change for them in five years and determined that they need to invest X amount of dollars. They have to trust me.

In a classic network engineering project, you sit down with a client, you ask a bunch of questions, and then you design a network based on the answers to those questions. But in wireless, you need

71

rapport with a customer—that's how you find out things that neither of you ever thought to ask. For instance, if someone tells me that they don't allow streaming video at their workplace, I'll design a network one way. However, if I learn through our extended conversations that actually there is nothing preventing employees from streaming video—that can be the difference between designing a network that works and designing one that doesn't work. I'm sort of like a detective or a doctor—I am diagnosing something but my patient doesn't always want to tell me the whole truth—or doesn't think the truth is really important. When I first come in, some customers are very guarded. They don't understand the technology and don't want to be taken advantage of. You have to break through that.

Q: What advice do you have for students who might be interested in this career?

A: Understand what you're getting into. If you don't have a passion for wireless, it's not the type of job you want to take. It can be challenging and rewarding, but it can also be extremely frustrating. If you're the type of person who is very by-the-book, if you like the predictability of math and you like it when one plus one equals two, you won't like wireless engineering. You have to spend as much time listening, talking, investigating, and looking at everything holistically as you do on the actual installation. It's a fascinating field, but it's not for everyone.

Other Jobs in Information Technology

3-D animator
Blogger
Computer gaming technical
  support specialist
Computer hardware engineer
Computer repair technician
Computer technology teacher
Computer scientist
Data entry operator
Data modeler
Desktop publisher
Graphic designer
Health informatics specialist
Help desk technician
Instructional designer
  (e-learning)
Internet marketer
IT manager

Mobile applications developer
Network administrator
Network architect
Network support specialist
Programmer
Robotics engineer
Search engine optimization
  (SEO) specialist
Technical writer
Telecommunication specialist
User experience specialist
Video game designer
Web content writer
Webmaster
Website administrator
Wi-Fi installer
Wireless communications
  technician

Editor's Note: The online *Occupational Outlook Handbook* of the US Department of Labor's Bureau of Labor Statistics is an excellent source of information on jobs in hundreds of career fields including many of those listed here. The *Occupational Outlook Handbook* may be accessed online at www.bls.gov/ooh/.

Index

Picture Credits

Maury Aaseng: 8

© Mike Blake/Reuters/Corbis: 28

© Jagadeesh Nv/epa/Corbis: 67

About the Author

Christine Wilcox writes fiction and nonfiction for young adults and adults. She has worked as an editor, an instructional designer, and a writing instructor. She lives in Richmond, Virginia, with her husband, David, and her son, Doug.